# JOURNEY TO THE WORLD'S EDGE

A Folk Tale in the Irish Tradition

A Play for Young Audiences

by

HARRY MICHAEL BAGDASIAN

and

ERNEST JOSELOVITZ

**Dramatic Publishing**
Woodstock, Illinois • England • Australia • New Zealand

## \*\*\* NOTICE \*\*\*

With love and admiration
we dedicate this script to our wives
Robbie McEwen and Elaine Zvonkin Joselovitz

## IMPORTANT BILLING AND CREDIT REQUIREMENTS

All producers of the play must give credit to the authors of the play in all programs distributed in connection with performances of the play and in all instances in which the title of the play appears for purposes of advertising, publicizing or otherwise exploiting the play and/or a production. The names of the authors must also appear on a separate line, on which no other name appears, immediately following the title, and must appear in size of type not less than fifty percent the size of the title type. Biographical information on the authors, if included in the playbook, may be used in all programs. In all programs this notice must appear:

"Produced by special arrangement with
DRAMATIC PUBLISHING COMPANY of Woodstock, Illinois"

## ACKNOWLEDGMENTS

*Journey to the World's Edge: A Folk Tale in the Irish Tradition* is the result of a commission from the Deaf Access Program at Imagination Stage, Bethesda, Maryland, which premiered the play January 27, 2007. The authors would like to thank the staff and cast who worked on the premier production of this play:

Imagination Stage Deaf Access Company Director & Production Director. . . . . . . . . . . . . . . . Lisa Agogliati

Actors . . . . . Tiasha Bera, Ilse Cruces, Emily Alpern Fisch, Brad Hammond, Ethan Joseph, Dahlia Levine, Saw Lowe, Ben Osborne, Leila Samara, Debra Segal, Sam Segal, Sarah Segal, Shanna Sorrells & Aria Warrick

Dramaturge . . . . . . . . . . . . . . . . . . . . . . . . . . . Kate Bryer

Visual Dramaturge. . . . . . . . . . . . . . . . . . Donna Salamoff

Sign Masters . . . . . . Su Robbins & Warren "Wawa" Snipe

Choreographer. . . . . . . . . . . . . . . . . . . . . . . . Fred Beam

Set Designer . . . . . . . . . . . . . Elizabeth Jenkins McFadden

Light Designer . . . . . . . . . . . . . . . . . . . . Ayun Fedorcha

Costume Designer . . . . . . . . . . . . . . . . . . . . Yvette Ryan

Props Designer . . . . . . . . . . . . . . . . . . . . Kathryn Pong

Stage Manager . . . . . . . . . . . . . . . . . . Wendy J. Calhoun

Assistant Stage Managers . . . . . . . . . . . . . Annie Dillon &
                                        Mulvenia Hemmings

Soundboard Operator . . . . . . . . . . . . . . . . . . Juely Siegel

Lightboard Operator . . . . . . . . . . . . . . . Wendy J. Calhoun

Photographer . . . . . . . . . . . . . . . . . . . . . . . Kate Mulligan

# JOURNEY TO THE WORLD'S EDGE
## A Folk Tale in the Irish Tradition

### CHARACTERS
(for a company of 24 players)

BRIGID SHAWN O'GRADY

and

A SEANACHAI
a circle of storytellers who play:

A Sage

Brigid's Mother
Brigid's Father - Michael Sean O'Grady

Shepherd
Street Cleaner
Schoolteacher
Baker
Tailor
Little Girl
Village Mother

Sea Mither
Kelpie

Farmer
Farmer's Wife
Giant (offstage voice) / Bog Serpent

Heron
Pine Marten

Seanachai 1 through 6

Suggested casting for a company of 14 players (keeping in mind that all are members of the "seanachai" or story circle):

Brigid
Sage / Body of Serpent
Brigid's Mother / Body of Serpent
Brigid's Father / Body of Serpent
Shepherd / Pine Marten
Street Cleaner / Giant Voice / Serpent
Schoolteacher / Heron
Baker / Seanachai 2 & 5
Tailor / Farmer's Wife / Body of Serpent
Little Girl / Body of Serpent
Village Mother / Sea Mither
Kelpie
Farmer / Seanachai 1 & 4
Heron / Seanachai 3 & 6

# JOURNEY TO THE WORLD'S EDGE
## A Folk Tale in the Irish Tradition


*Lights come up on a vast, nearly empty and quiet place. Think empty stage, for now. It is, after all, the world's edge (though no one knows that yet). It's pretty stark except for a small pond of water ringed by river stones.*

*In this vast near emptiness stands BRIGID Shawn O'Grady, an Irish farm lass of about twelve, who is intently staring at a stick in her hand. It is a Bard's Rod. We readily notice that she is wearing an oddly shaped boot, and, once she paces in agitation, it is obvious that she has a deformed foot. Away from her, unseen by BRIGID, but obvious to us, is a robed and hooded figure. BRIGID doesn't acknowledge his presence. The silence is only broken when BRIGID chants...*

BRIGID. "Tap once, twice, thrice/ Bard's Rod, point the way to the Well at World's Edge/ to what I need/ point the way."

*(She twirls around until the rod, like the needle of a compass, points across the stage at the robed and hooded figure. BRIGID is amazed. The picture is held, then...)*

BRIGID. You! You're the Sage!

SAGE. I am the Sage you seek. Welcome, Brigid Shawn O'Grady.

BRIGID. You know my name?

SAGE. And your destiny.

BRIGID. To change this misshapen foot of mine to be like my other, and like everyone else's.

SAGE. 'Tis only left for you to tell your tale to me. A seanachai [sheh-na'-quee] I summon then, a circle of storytellers, to help tell your tale. We begin as all real-life stories do…with a question.

*(A SEANACHAI, a circle of storytellers, enters. This includes the rest of the cast.)*

SEANACHAI 1. Why did you leave?

SEANACHAI 2. Why did you leave?

SEANACHAI/ALL. Why did you leave the house, your home?

*(The SAGE takes the Bard's Rod and hands it to the first SEANACHAI who enters followed by the rest of the SEANACHAI. BRIGID backs into the center of their semicircle and faces the audience as the SEANACHAI begins the story, passing the Bard's Rod one to another [BRIGID and the others speak to the audience].)*

BRIGID. That little girl I saw passing our home, one day then the next and every day. That little girl carrying those books, where is she going?

MRS O'GRADY. ...Brigid would ask me, her mother. "To school," I would tell her.

BRIGID. "School." 'Twas a new word for me. "*I* want to go to school."

FATHER. ...She would insist to me, her father. "'Tis best you stay at home," I told her.

MRS O'GRADY. "We keep you here at home for your own good," I said. "You're different, Brigid."

BRIGID. "I am?" I asked. *(A brief silence.)*

MRS O'GRADY. "Here at home," I did explain, "Here at home, you're safe."

FATHER. "You'll learn from your mother... About numbers and words," I told her.

BRIGID. I got my own book, *this* book— I learned to read with it...dreamy tales of faraway adventures.

MRS O'GRADY. She read it over and over, 'til the pages were worn.

LITTLE GIRL. Day after day Brigid would see me, a little girl, pass the O'Grady cottage on my way to the village.

BRIGID. What is a "village"?

SEANACHAI 1. ...Brigid would think...

BRIGID. Is it like my book?

*(The SEANACHAI continue...)*

SEANACHAI 2. And years went by.

SEANACHAI 3. Brigid grew up inside her world of four walls...

SEANACHAI 4. ...one window and the door locked...

SEANACHAI 5. ...reading her one book.

BRIGID *(reading from the book)*. "…and the wish was granted. So the Sea Mither smiled, and disappeared again into the ocean waves."

SEANACHAI 1. Grown restless…

SEANACHAI 2. …thinking always…

BRIGID. What's a "school"? A "village"?

SEANACHAI 3. Then, all in one day…

SEANACHAI 4. …she saw passing by a cartful of colorful cloth and silks…

SEANACHAI 5. …and a farmer walking home from the village carrying a stack of baked bread.

SEANACHAI 6. And a shepherd with a bundle of sheep's wool tied to his horse.

BRIGID. A school? A village? There's colorful silks in the village, and woolens and baked bread and schoolbooks and what else. What else? A place of mysteries and wonder. I must see for myself what the little girl sees every day.

*(While the dialogue/storytelling continues, the SEANA-CHAI begin to set up simple set pieces and props to create a village. Various SEANACHAI take up simple props and/or costume pieces to become a SHEPHERD, a SCHOOLTEACHER, a TAILOR, a VILLAGE MOTHER, a BAKER and a STREET CLEANER.)*

BRIGID. So one morning, before the sun had risen…

SEANACHAI/ALL. …when everything was gray…

BRIGID. …and oh-so-quiet. Not a soul was in sight.

SEANACHAI/ALL. Not a soul.

BRIGID. My mother and father asleep…I escaped…and for the first time in my walking talking life…

SEANACHAI/ALL. ...the first time in her walking talking life...

BRIGID. I left the house that confined me since infancy.

SEANACHAI/ALL. ...From the house that had confined her...

BRIGID. I'd not been allowed, since a babe, upon the streets of Kilfenora.

SHEPHERD. Never walked on the village green.

BRIGID. And there was the schoolhouse I'd not ever been inside; I peeked through...

SEANACHAI/ALL. Peeked through...

BRIGID. Rows of wooden desks!

SCHOOLTEACHER. With their inkwells and books, a world of maps upon the walls.

BRIGID. How could a place so wonderful be bad for me?

SEANACHAI/ALL. ...She went to the bake shop.

BAKER. ...Gazing at my soda bread in the window, and yesterday's dainty cakes.

SEANACHAI/ALL. To the tailor's shop.

TAILOR. Oh, and she was dazzled by the bright red dress there, and the feathered hats.

SEANACHAI/ALL. Before she knew it, the sun was up...

STREET CLEANER. And I was up.

TAILOR/BAKER/TEACHER. And so were many of us.

LITTLE GIRL *(approaches BRIGID)*. Hi, what's your name? My name is Brianna.

BRIGID. Oh. I need be going home.

LITTLE GIRL. Want to play with me? *(Her mother rushes up and grabs Brianna away.)*

VILLAGE MOTHER. Keep your distance, little one! Can't you see?...IT?

BRIGID. What?

VILLAGE MOTHER *(pointing at BRIGID's foot). That!*

LITTLE GIRL. Ooh, ooh! *(Wanting to touch it:)* Does it hurt?

VILLAGE MOTHER *(pulling her child away).* She's that infant that's grown up now. The one with that ugly foot!

BRIGID. My foot?

*(The VILLAGERS turn their backs on BRIGID; they never address BRIGID directly.)*

VILLAGE MOTHER *(to the others).* That affliction! Her frightening difference.

BRIGID. 'Tis not my fault, ma'am.

SHEPHERD *(to the others).* Got a hoof, like a sheep.

SCHOOLTEACHER *(to the others).* Poor thing...twisted on the outside and inside.

BRIGID. 'Tis nothing I've done.

BAKER *(to the others).* That foot—what a frightening mistake.

TAILOR *(to the others).* She's impossible to properly clothe. With that foot, not pretty at all.

SHEPHERD *(to the others).* A monster.

*(The STREET CLEANER spits on the ground BRIGID's walked on and washes it "clean.")*

BAKER *(to the others).* She's different

TAILOR *(to the others).* She's ugly.

BRIGID. What have I done?

STREET CLEANER *(to the others).* She doesn't belong.

SHEPHERD *(to the others).* Do you see her?

SCHOOLTEACHER *(to the others).* I don't.

BAKER *(to the others)*. Not me.

BRIGID. Why won't you look at me?

TAILOR *(to the others)*. Someone that ugly…

STREET CLEANER *(to the others)*. …that strange…

BRIGID. I am?

SCHOOLTEACHER *(to the others)*. …she should go away…

SHEPHERD *(to the others)*. …Disappear like she's never been here.

BRIGID *(humiliated)*. I wish I could.

BAKER *(to the others)*. …I don't see her.

TAILOR *(to the others)*. I never saw her.

ALL THE OTHER VILLAGERS. Me neither.

BRIGID. Stop…stop…stop!

*(Brigid's FATHER strides through the hostile circle, pushing aside one of them, then another, to his daughter, now huddled on the ground.)*

FATHER. I'm here. We're going home. *(Silenced by his look, the circle moves slowly away. Her FATHER lifts her in his arms, carries her away.)*

VILLAGE MOTHER. Shame on you, Michael Sean O'Grady!

*(As they back away, reforming their storytellers' circle…)*

LITTLE GIRL *(sadly)*. Where's she going?

VILLAGE MOTHER. Who? The girl? Pretend she was never here.

SEANACHAI. And Brigid's father carried her away…

SEANACHAI. …to the safe confines of their home.

*(He's carried her into their home, met there by an alarmed MOTHER.)*

BRIGID'S MOTHER *(feeling her for any injuries)*. They've not hurt you, my joy, my blessing, Mother's angel.

BRIGID. They stared...they mocked me.

FATHER. You've been told, time and again, not to leave this house. One time is one too many.

MOTHER. It's for your own good, don't you see now?

BRIGID. But they do not know me.

MOTHER. They were frightened by your foot when you were a babe in my arms. For them nothing has changed.

FATHER. Now you know the cruel truth of the world.

MOTHER. You've a life here, inside the four walls. You'll be sweeping the floor, like any other day, and later we'll read a tale from the book.

FATHER *(taking the book)*. Not ever again! It's this book she's learned to read. Filling her mind with fictions, made for false hopes and restlessness. Tales told by liars and lunatics. There is no magic in this world, no fairy fishes and ponies flying over pretty-colored rainbows! *(He tosses the book away.)*

BRIGID. No-o-o-o!!

FATHER. It's for the best, child. You will not leave here again to be hurt again. Nor read another wild tale. You'll be rid of that book. *(He leaves.)*

BRIGID. This foot! *(She throws down the broom.)* This foot! This foot! I hate this foot!

MOTHER. You're our one child; for us every part of you is precious.

BRIGID. This is no longer home to me, 'tis a prison. This foot is the cause of it all.

MOTHER. Those others will never see what's inside.

BRIGID. What's inside is useless if I can't be like everyone else! I want to be free to walk about and go to school!

MOTHER. It's not to be.

*(BRIGID retrieves the book, sits with it held tight in her lap. Her MOTHER holds out her hand to take the book. BRIGID clings to it.)*

BRIGID. You'll not be taking my book from me. There is!—there is!—hope and magic somewhere in the world. *(Opening the book.)* Here's the gentle caring Sea Mither, who might appear to those who ask, and answer wishes. A true story surely.

MOTHER. No, darlin', wishes fly no further than the pages of the book, like dreams in a wake-up world. *(Hands her the broom.)* There's the chores to do. *(She takes a bucket, leaving.)* The book cannot be here when your father returns. You'll see to it.

BRIGID *(now alone, reading)*. "The Sea Mither appears over the Cliffs of Moher, a barren place high above the ocean, where but few dare travel." But not so far from here, only past Liscannor and Doolin.

SEANACHAI/ALL *(alternately in Gaelic)*. Magic is here. Ta' draichot anseo.

BRIGID. Magic is there.

SEANACHAI/ALL. Hope is here. Ta' dochas anseo.

BRIGID. My only hope is there. Fare thee well, Mother, Father... *(steps back from it all)* house o' my birth and my childhood. 'Til I return the way I ought to be. *(And BRIGID turns and goes.)*

*(As they chant, the SEANACHAI combine movement with small set pieces to indicate BRIGID's travel and her ultimate destination.)*

SEANACHAI/ALL.
> There is magic in the depths and in the waves.
> There is magic in the wetness of the water, and the
>   coldness.
> There is magic in the blueness and the taste and the
>   smell of the sea.

*(She is at the very edge of the Cliffs of Moher overlooking—700 feet below—the vast ocean.)*

BRIGID. Sea Mither! I do stand before you!...high above the sea, on the Cliffs of Moher... Hear me! I was born with this difference, unlike everyone else. I hate this body of mine which is made ugly and weak. I hate this head of mine which is made confused. I hate this heart of mine which feels only anger and despair. Sea Mither! Bring me your magic! Sea Mither! Bring me your hope!

*(The Bard's Rod is being passed from one SEANACHAI member to another, until...)*

SEANACHAI/ALL.
> Magic is here. Ta' draichot anseo.
> Hope is here. Ta' dochas anseo.

*(...it is handed to the SEA MITHER who has has risen from the "ocean" before the child.)*

BRIGID. Oh my. Oh my.

*(...and speaks:)*

SEA MITHER. Child, I hear your cry. Tell me your wish.

BRIGID. I want this one foot of mine to be like the other, and like everyone else's. You'll change how people look upon me, and they'll like me, they will. Change this ugly foot of mine—please! please!

SEA MITHER. Three be the number of tests, and then you'll reach a person for wishes asked and wisely answered.

BRIGID. And you're not the person? Why not?

SEA MITHER. There's more to a wish than the wishing. You need to show yourself worthy. A hard way, a testing way. Do you dare?

BRIGID. I'll do what needs the doing.

SEA MITHER. Ah then, you'll take this Bard's Rod. *(BRIGID does.)* Breathe deep now, look to where the sea meets the sky, listen to the waves upon the rocks far below. Hold this Bard's Rod high! I can only help you help yourself. It will point the way. The rest is up to you. You are to use these words...

SEA MITHER & THE SEANACHAI. Tap once, twice, thrice/ Bard's Rod, point the way to the Well at World's Edge/ Point the way to what I need/ Point the way.

*(BRIGID twirls around until the Bard's Rod, like the needle of a compass, points straight out over the cliff.)*

SEA MITHER. Follow it you must, without a swerve or a curve.

BRIGID. But...but... *(She drops it to the ground.)* It points out over the cliff.

SEA MITHER. Follow it you must, through three tests, follow it you must and prove yourself worthy.

SEANACHAI/ALL. Magic is here. Hope is here.

BRIGID. I...cannot. I'll be drowned, or my bones broken on the rocks below.

SEA MITHER. Follow it, to the Well at World's Edge.

SEANACHAI/ALL. Magic is here. Hope is here.

*(BRIGID hesitantly picks up the rod and it points again, out over the cliffside.)*

SEANACHAI/ALL. There's magic here.

BRIGID. The magic is real.

SEANACHAI/ALL. And hope!

BRIGID. And hope is all I have!

*(And she spreads her arms and lets herself fall off the cliff! The SEANACHAI...as directed by SEA MITHER, catch BRIGID and carry her "into the sea.")*

BRIGID. Water, oh 'tis cold but dry like make-believe. I'm swimming or being carried or can I be dreaming it all?

SEANACHAI/ALL. Tumbling over and over.

BRIGID. Up or down or side to side, it seems all the same; North is South or West, left is right or am I wrong?

SEANACHAI/ALL. Spinning 'round and 'round.

BRIGID. A minute's gone by, perhaps a day, seems almost forever, or is it no more than the blink of an eye?

SEANACHAI/ALL. Slipping and sliding, floating or flying...

BRIGID. Is that a shark or a mermaid? A dolphin or a sea fairy?

SEANACHAI 1. Until she finds herself on a sandy beach at the edge of the sea.

*(SFX: the gentle sound of waves continues under as...directed by SEA MITHER, the SEANACHAI set BRIGID down and reform their storytellers' circle.)*

SEANACHAI 2. Three is the number of tests and then you'll reach a person for wishes asked and wisely answered.

*(BRIGID is now on what seems an abandoned beach, upon which lies what appears to be a single rock. BRIGID, looking about in bewilderment...)*

BRIGID. Where in the world... Where *out* of the world, am I?

SEANACHAI/ALL. A world of wondrous adventures and mysteries.

BRIGID. 'Tis a lonely place this barren beach.

SEA MITHER. Her first test, then—what...shall...it be?

*(BRIGID sits upon the "rock." Only to have it, quite alive, spin around to reveal itself as a KELPIE, sitting, hogtied and enraged with frustration.)*

BRIGID. Oh! So sorry.

KELPIE. Sorry? For plunking your lumpy little self upon the singular body of the one the only the supreme Kelpie?

BRIGID. Kelpie?

KELPIE. Do I look like a chair to you?

BRIGID. Do let me help…

KELPIE. Oh! Ah! You!—do actually think I need your help? I am strong!—I am swift!—I am smart! Ten fierce…twenty fierce demons, with weapons galore—knives and axes, sharp and magical—thirty fierce and sneaky demons attacked me all-a-sudden…and from behind…and in the dark. And…and… And a spell was put upon me, that's what it was, a momentary mortifying paralysis.

BRIGID. How long have you been…

KELPIE. Days…nights…weeks and weeks… *(He momentarily collapses, but then he's again struggling with his ropes.)* I'll be free…of this…impediment… NOW! …NOW!

BRIGID. If you'll but be still…I can…

KELPIE. Oh! Ah! *(Trying to loosen his ties:)* You…dare help me…you mushy-hearted mealy-minded fluttery buttery…*human*! A slip…here! A dip…there! A zig…and a zag and…I'll…be… *(He fails yet again.)* You had better go on your way, lass, I can but warn you, for when I snap this trap—and I will!—in less than a minute!—and my hoofs be free, I am nasty, I cannot help myself, I am almighty mean, I am!

*(The KELPIE faints, exhausted. BRIGID steps back, looks down at him. SEANACHAI 1, 2 and 3 step forward to observe and tell us what BRIGID is thinking.)*

BRIGID. I'll be gone, I shall. *(But she stops, and bending over him, reconsiders.)* Oh my, the poor dear. *(She pulls back, away.)*

SEANACHAI 1. He's a Kelpie…

SEANACHAI 2. …she reminds herself.

SEANACHAI 3. You know what they say about kelpies.

BRIGID. A hateful trickster…

SEANACHAI 1. …and nasty with his every word.

BRIGID. He'll trick me.

SEANACHAI 2. …she thinks to herself.

SEANACHAI 3. He'll hurt me.

BRIGID. Oh, but he's tied up and so tired.

SEANACHAI 2 & 3. Why he'll surely die.

SEANACHAI 1. Let him.

SEANACHAI 2. Leave him.

SEANACHAI 3. Forget him.

BRIGID. Why, he'll surely die.

SEANACHAI 1. And then she decided.

BRIGID. I can't—no, no—I can't bring myself to leave him to die.

*(And she unties him. There is a silence. The KELPIE groans, and then slowly feels the freedom of his limbs. With her eyes upon him, BRIGID backs away, but not very quickly. Suddenly…)*

KELPIE. Oh! Ah! Free! *(And he's up, jumping and laughing, until he sees her there.)* I was one minute away from freeing myself. Isn't that what it looked like to you?

BRIGID. Oh. Uh. Surely.

KELPIE. A spell—an unbreakable, paralyzing spell…that *I* broke. Another first, another legendary feat for the Kelpie. *(Shuffles around.)* Zip zap hip hop swing swoop! *(Offering his bicep for her to…)* Feel that…feel it! *(She puts one finger on his "arm.")* Uh?—strength. I could hit you and kick you and bite you until it hurts. I could I could I could!

BRIGID. I'll be on my way then.

KELPIE. Do you know where you are? Don't answer that. Why am I talking to you? You are totally insignificant. Humans are so…strange: next-to-nothing nose and ears—ugh! Hands and feet that don't match—ugh! Not enough hair to cover yourself. Soft, slow, and, in your case, KIND! No use denyin' it! *(He shakes his head in utter disgust.)* And then you've got that sore ankle there.

BRIGID. It is, actually, my misshapen foot. It's forever. That's why…

KELPIE. Oh. *(Comparing.)* Looks like mine. Pretty. But, except for the pretty foot, you are…well, *human*. *(Showing himself off, dancing around again.)* Beautiful legs!—beautiful eyes!—me me me!—beautiful me! Zip zap hip hop swing swoop. *(Stops.)* You'll never make it. Do you know where you're going?

BRIGID. Wherever this points me.

KELPIE. Oh. Ah. The Bard's Rod, that. Go on, point it then.

BRIGID/SEANACHAI. Tap once, twice, thrice/ Bard's Rod, point the way to the Well at World's Edge/ Point the way to what I need/ Point the way.

*(BRIGID twirls around until the rod points…)*

KELPIE. Well it's pointing in the general direction of the Well at World's Edge, where sits an old man, the Sage. *(Again, BRIGID is about to leave.)* Don't beg. I'll help you.

BRIGID. You?! No! No! Why would I want the help of a nasty, rubbish-mouth Kelpie?

KELPIE. Why? Because, you're a hopeless hapless human. Because, with all the hardships you're bound to face—this is a chance to make me famous. You'll be a witness to greatness. Wanna ride wanna ride wanna ride?

BRIGID. I've read that the Kelpie tricks riders out to the darkest depths of the sea.

KELPIE. You have? Oh. That must be my cousin. *(He stands, his back bent for her, in invitation. But she hesitates.)* Well now, 'tis only a prank, with not much drowning. *(Still hesitant.)* I promise, no sea-dunking, no river-plunking. *(She climbs aboard. She then points her Bard's Rod. And the KELPIE rides her offstage.)* "And the brave Kelpie, swift and strong," 'tis to be written, "carried the helpless young lass on her quest over the rocky shore…"

*(As directed by SEA MITHER, the SEANACHAI come to life, describing the journey as they set simple props and don costume pieces for the next scene. KELPIE reenters with BRIGID on his back.)*

SEANACHAI 1. Climbing high.

SEANACHAI 2. Past what seem like wild goats grazing and frolicsome rabbits.

SEANACHAI 3. Is that goat blue?

BRIGID. Did that rabbit snarl at me and wink?
SEANACHAI 1. Climbing high.
BRIGID. No boys are here, nor another girl in sight.
SEANACHAI 2. The sun is red.
SEANACHAI 3. The stars are a-twinkling.
SEANACHAI 1. Climbing higher.
BRIGID. Is that the roar of the ocean I hear? *(The KELPIE carries BRIGID offstage.)*
SEANACHAI 2. The hot wind of the desert she feels?
SEANACHAI 3. High high into the hills of Connemara.
SEANACHAI 1. 'Twas a long journey... A tiring journey from the sea to a vast countryside...

*(Starlight. Reentering, BRIGID now carrying the KELPIE, who is asleep. Tired and limping, she's using the Bard's Rod as a cane. She lowers the KELPIE.)*

SEANACHAI 2. Fields of grazing sheep. Field after field of farmland...
BRIGID. A farm.
KELPIE. A barn.
BRIGID. Where we could rest.

*(The FARMER and his WIFE enter.)*

BRIGID *(bumping into FARMER)*. Oh.
FARMER. Middle of the night, and you're in my farmyard.
BRIGID. I'm on a quest.
FARMER'S WIFE. A quest?
FARMER. Oh sure.
BRIGID. My foot.

KELPIE. It's a pretty little Kelpie-like foot, as far as I'm concerned, but she...

FARMER. You, you're a Kelpie. A Kelpie is trouble. Go away.

FARMER'S WIFE *(urging him aside, speaks to KELPIE and BRIGID)*. You must be cold.

KELPIE. And tired. She's awfully tired.

*(WIFE gently places a square of hay under KELPIE's head. Then, another, pillowing BRIGID's head as she tells them...)*

FARMERS WIFE. You're welcome, travelers, for the night. 'Tis only hay for a pillow in the barn of our humble farm.

*(FARMER and his WIFE exit. BRIGID and the KELPIE sleep.)*

SEANACHAI 1. Sunlight. The sound of sheep. A rooster crows. 'Tis morning.

*(Brief silence. Suddenly, the sleeping BRIGID and KELPIE are "bounced" to the sound of a huge thumping footstep. [NOTE: every "step" the GIANT takes is indicated by the cast reacting as if the very earth beneath them moves—we'll call it a "bounce."] By the third thumping bounce, they're both awake and standing. The FARMER'S WIFE lunges onstage, aproned, with a frying pan in hand—there are four griddlecakes in the pan. She is followed by her husband, the FARMER,*

*wearing a napkin, carrying a fork, and balancing a plateful of griddlecakes.)*

FARMER'S WIFE/KELPIE. A Giant!
FARMER. Aaah!

*(Just then, another thumping "bounce." They all look behind them and up and up...and up.)*

FARMER'S WIFE *(almost whispering)*. H-h-h-help.
BRIGID. Oh...my.
FARMER. I'll not leave my breakfast behind!
FARMER'S WIFE. *You'll* be the breakfast, m'dear.
FARMER. What's a Giant doing in our neighborhood? Never in my lifetime!
SEANACHAI 2. Suddenly...a big splash! *(Everyone bounces.)*
FARMER'S WIFE *(pointing DL)*. His one foot is past that hill, where McNamara's pond used to be.
SEANACHAI 3. And then...a splintering crash! *(Everyone bounces)* ...and flying feathers!
BRIGID *(pointing UL)*. His other foot is over there, where your chicken coop used to be.
SEANACHAI 1. From high up, they heard the voice of the Giant...
GIANT'S VOICE *(from a distance)*. Hahaha! Squish! Squash! Fun fun fun!
BRIGID. 'Tis a test, surely.
KELPIE. Ah, well then. I'll not be interfering. 'Til you fail. Giant: big and strong and ugly. You: little and weak and ugly.

BRIGID. I cannot hope to fight him. Oh but I must do *something*.

KELPIE. To be sure, you did untie a knot or two in freeing me, and you did carry me a few feet...yards...miles.

BRIGID. I did indeed.

*(Another thud, the earth bounces. And another...and a large menacing shadow overhead. The echoing voice of the GIANT is heard from high above.)*

GIANT. Hi, little people! I'm going to step on you and you and you and you, and kill you and suck upon your tiny bones!

BRIGID. Truly, you don't want to do that.

GIANT. I do. 'Tis fun. You'll go squish, squirt and squash and be dead. Hahaha.

BRIGID. If you do that, my father will have to kill *you*. He'll soon be home, he will.

KELPIE. Your father?!

BRIGID. My father...the giant.

FARMER. Her father's a giant?

FARMER'S WIFE *(shrugging)*. No harm letting him above think so.

BRIGID. He's truly a giant among giants, is my father.

GIANT. Bigger than me? Hahaha.

BRIGID. Oh, surely. I myself shall be your small size...in about two weeks.

GIANT. Two weeks? Well now, how old might *you* be?

BRIGID. Seven days old.

GIANT. But you talk and walk and...

KELPIE. ...seven days old!

BRIGID. In a week I'll be higher than those trees.

KELPIE. In *three* weeks she'll be tall as that mountain over there.

*(They all nod enthusiastically, carefully looking up at the GIANT. He's thinking—sort of.)*

GIANT. I don't believe you. So I'll stomp on you now, and squash you flat just for the fun of it.

KELPIE. Stop!

FARMER'S WIFE. No!

BRIGID. Griddlecakes!

FARMER/KELPIE/GIANT. Huh?

BRIGID. For breakfast! We've been making these griddle-cakes...

FARMER *(to his WIFE)*. *My* griddlecakes, for *my* breakfast.

BRIGID. ...for my giant father's giant breakfast.

FARMER. What is she talking about? We've neither one of us seen a Giant in our whole lifetime.

*(Meanwhile, BRIGID is rapidly grabbing the horseshoes from off the unwilling KELPIE.)*

KELPIE. Ouch! Ooh! My shoe! Give me back my shoe!

BRIGID. It's metal. I'm in need of metal.

KELPIE. No! Oh! Not that one, too!

FARMER. Why are you putting a horseshoe...

KELPIE. My shoes!

FARMER. In my griddlecakes?

BRIGID. You'll see. *(She stuffs the horseshoes into two of the griddlecakes. To the GIANT:)* He eats about a hundred of these griddlecakes...specially made for the giant of giants.

GIANT. Special giant's griddlecakes? I like griddlecakes. I want one.

BRIGID. Oh, I couldn't do that.

GIANT. Yes you can, yes you will, yes, yes, yes, you better or else!

BRIGID. They're specially tough, the way my father likes them. *(BRIGID holds out the griddlecake. No one moves. Finally, the KELPIE takes it.)*

KELPIE. I'll...do...it. *(Creeps toward offstage, and the GIANT.)* I am b-brave.

BRIGID. You are very brave.

KELPIE. I am very b-brave...I am very b-brave... *(Turning to them.)* Oooh! His hand is as big as a bear! *(He takes the griddlecake from BRIGID, goes offstage to hand it to the GIANT. The others watch this action, commenting...)*

FARMER'S WIFE. He's taken the griddlecake...

FARMER. He's popping my griddlecake into his mouth...

*(KELPIE returns to the group. A few seconds, then...)*

GIANT. Ouch! My tooth!

*(...and a very large tooth comes tumbling down.)*

BRIGID. Strange. That's what he eats every morning, dozens and dozens.

GIANT. That father of yours must be very...

KELPIE. Tough as iron.

BRIGID. I'm truly sorry. Here's my own griddlecakes, you'll see, soft enough for my own young self. *(She bites into one of the remaining on the pile:)* Try one of these then, soft enough for me. *(She hands KELPIE the second "loaded" griddlecake.)*

KELPIE. Oh no. Again? I am b-brave.

BRIGID. You are very brave.

KELPIE. I am very b-brave... *(KELPIE leaves with the second griddlecake.)*

FARMER'S WIFE. He's taken the griddlecake...

FARMER. *My* griddlecake.

FARMER'S WIFE. ...he's popping it into his mouth...

*(The KELPIE returns to the group as...)*

GIANT. Ouch!

*(...and another tooth comes tumbling into sight.)*

GIANT. You're a family tough ath oak treeth. H-how big ith thish father of yourth?

BRIGID. He's so big that on his way from the other side of the world to breakfast here, so that we'll have a sunshiny morn, he reaches up and taps the sun itself ahead of him. There he is now!

GIANT. Oh. Ah.

KELPIE. Isn't that the very top of his head I see?

BRIGID. Mornin', Dad! Your griddlecakes be on the griddle! griddlecakes—griddle—hurry!

GIANT. Maybe I should be leaving. I'd not be dith-turbing a fellow gianth's morning meal.

BRIGID. There's breakfast every morning. You're welcome to come back.

GIANT. No thank you! I am never coming thith way ever again!

*(A series of hurried earth-bouncing thumps quickly diminishing into the distance—and their bounces reflect their diminished intensity. Stunned silence of relief.)*

BRIGID. He's gone

FARMER'S WIFE. The Giant was so frightened by the tale you told, surely he won't ever return.

FARMER. I'll be eating what's left of my breakfast then. *(He does so.)*

FARMER'S WIFE. Well done, lass!

BRIGID. Your chicken coop is in ruins.

FARMER'S WIFE. But our lives are not, because of you! Smartness it took, to fool a foolish giant. Thanks, me darlin' girl!

*(The FARMER and his WIFE exit with the teeth and the griddlecakes. BRIGID and the KELPIE are alone.)*

BRIGID *(very happy)*. We've become quite a frightful team, Kelpie.

KELPIE. It was you who did it.

BRIGID. I did! We'll be going then. Kelpie? *(She holds out the Bard's Rod and begins the chant.)* Tap once, twice, thrice/ Bard's Rod, point...

KELPIE *(interrupting her chant)*. You'll be going. I'll be waiting here for new shoes. *(Demonstrating, he hops gingerly upon his "feet.")* Ooh, ouch, pretty pretty feet, delicate and tender, ooh, ouch!

BRIGID. But, I cannot, without you, Kelpie.

KELPIE. I suppose that's true enough. You'd not have smartly fooled that Giant without my standing beside you as an intimidating warning to the brute.

BRIGID. You! You did nothing!

KELPIE. No? So? Are you telling me, then, you did it all? All by yourself?

BRIGID. Well I did now, didn't I?

KELPIE. Test of three, you told me.

BRIGID. That's true.

KELPIE. It's two tests you've now passed.

BRIGID. What?!

KELPIE. I was the first test.

BRIGID. You?

KELPIE. A test of your heart. My being nasty, threatened your very life, but you untied me, didn't you—and be-friended me along the way.

BRIGID. You, a test?

KELPIE. Indeed, I was the first of your three tests. And the Giant was, for certain, another.

BRIGID. But now…

KELPIE. Be gone to the final test that awaits you.

BRIGID. Go alone?…another test? It's too hard.

KELPIE. You want that wish of yours answered?

BRIGID. I will.

*(She goes to the rod to begin the chant, but stops, goes to the KELPIE and gives him a hug. He tightly closes his eyes, in a fake show of utter disgust until she's on her way. SEA MITHER rises up, "directs" the transition*

*as the SEANACHAI use movement and props and maybe
simple set pieces to effect BRIGID's travels and her next
destination.)*

BRIGID. Tap once, twice, thrice/ Bard's Rod, point the
way to the Well at World's Edge/ Point the way to what
I need/ Point the way.

SEANACHAI 1. She walked...

SEANACHAI 2. And walked...

SEANACHAI 3. And walked.

SEANACHAI 4. One little girl in a land of talking animals,
giants and flying fairies. And she's thinking...

BRIGID. Everyone here will see my foot, and the difference, and the ugliness.

SEANACHAI 5. But...in *this* world, no one did.

SEANACHAI 6. She's got no wings, no feathers.

SEANACHAI/ALL. 'Tis one of those humans.

SEANACHAI 1. No scales, no fins.

SEANACHAI 2. No stripes on her, no spots of any kind.

SEANACHAI/ALL. One of those humans.

SEANACHAI 3. No fur, no tail.

SEANACHAI 4. So big...

SEANACHAI 5. So small...

SEANACHAI 6. So covered up...

SEANACHAI 1. And what's that in your hand?

BRIGID. The Bard's Rod.

SEANACHAI 1. Ah that—the well...

SEANACHAI 2. The old man...the Sage...

SEANACHAI 3. A wish to make.

SEANACHAI 4. A wish for what?

BRIGID *(showing it)*. This foot of mine.

SEANACHAI 5 *(puzzled)*. Foot? What about it?

BRIGID. But don't you see?—'tis different from my other one.

SEANACHAI 6 *(shrugging to the others)*. That's not the way they're supposed to be?

SEANACHAI 1. That's hardly strange at all.

SEANACHAI 2. A flying fairy—now that's strange.

SEANACHAI 3. A Giant is very strange.

BRIGID. I'd thought: They'll see my foot and the difference and the ugliness.

SEANACHAI/ALL. But: in *this* world, no one did.

SEANACHAI 4. Rest awhile with us.

SEANACHAI 5. Take a bite or two of this.

SEANACHAI 6. And this.

*(They give her some food, she continues walking, eating and then stops.)*

SEANACHAI 1. There it was...stretching from here to the horizon and maybe beyond...a bog, dark and wet.

*(From the SEANACHAI, sounds of frogs and animals rustling in the bordering sedge and leatherleaf. They drop back into their story circle, yet continue their vocal underscoring as the scene plays out.)*

BRIGID. 'Tis pointing straight ahead, surely to the Well at World's Edge. But without a curve or a swerve through that muck and mud.

*(A dignified HERON approaches her, as does a young otter-like PINE MARTEN.)*

HERON. There is no way 'round.

BRIGID. 'Tis a heron saying words to me? 'Tis a world of wonders, with creatures that talk...like pages lifted from my book of tales.

HERON. When human children come here...

MARTEN. All think "Hey, 'tis mighty strange." *(Each shrugs at the other.)*

BRIGID. Others have been here before me?

HERON. Children only.

MARTEN. Been here but no further. Not one.

HERON. And across this bog is the only way to the Well at World's Edge.

BRIGID. 'Tis my third test. I must make it past the slime and stink of that peat moss and mud.

MARTEN. Mud mud, ooh, I love mud!— For jumping and diving, swimming and splashing and playing, the slick and so slimy muck and the mud! *(About to dive right in:)* Mud, mud, ooh, I love mud!

HERON. And the Serpent.

BRIGID. Serpent?

MARTEN *(screeches to a halt, backs away from bog)*. Ah, the...the Serpent. No fun at all.

HERON. 'Tis a terrible fierce Serpent.

MARTEN. Who likes us Martens...for breakfast. Evil. Evil through and through, from head to tail.

HERON. Many others have been here before you. And every one has run away in fright.

MARTEN. There was that one, frozen in fear...

HERON. Legend has it, she was lunch.

MARTEN. 'Tis the Bog Serpent you must tame. The Bog Serpent guards this place and the Well at World's Edge that's beyond.

HERON. The legend says grab its tongue...

MARTEN. Oh surely, lots o' luck. The tongue needs to be grabbed. It's in his mouth.

HERON. Past his terrible poisonous fangs!

*(A huge SERPENT's head appears just above the slimy surface, far away. The SERPENT is to be played by as many of the story circle as desired.)*

BRIGID. I cannot!

HERON. Then be gone and that's the end of it.

BRIGID. Oh, but it does look large and terrible.

MARTEN *(indicating it)*. You need to stand on this serpent's rock.

BRIGID. I cannot, with this weak and twisted foot of mine.

HERON. Does it not make the other foot stronger?

BRIGID *(as she steps up on the rock)*. Well... Oh, but such a small rock, and slippery besides.

HERON. Are your *thoughts* small? Do your *feelings* slip and slide?

BRIGID *(trying her balance while voicing her determination)*. I will...have...this foot of mine mended.

MARTEN. You'd better not move, that's the only way.

HERON. He's a touchy sort of monster.

MARTEN. A moody type.

BRIGID. I will have an ordinary foot...like ordinary children.

HERON. Any movement...

MARTEN. A twitch or an itch...

HERON. The smallest of sounds...

MARTEN. A moan or a groan.

HERON. And—quick—he'll sting you into frozen submission!

MARTEN. ...and eat you whole.

BRIGID. I can be still. I can be quiet. *(She doesn't move another muscle.)* The tongue will tame him.

*(The SERPENT reappears, closer, rising higher from the bog and disappears again.)*

HERON. This is when that wee girl with red hair ran away shrieking.

*(The SERPENT reappears closer still, higher still, above the bog, showing its terrible poisonous fangs now, and hissing loudly.)*

MARTEN. This is when that tall and mighty boy shivered, eyes wide, he stumbled and jumped and crawled away.

*(The SERPENT appears now in its full height right before the girl.)*

HERON/MARTEN. This is when...*WE* RUN AWAY! Aah! Aah! Aah! *(They do indeed.)*

*(BRIGID is alone now, on the rock, stock still and alert, as the SERPENT slinks to her...)*

SEANACHAI 1. I will not move, she thought.

SEANACHAI 2. The Serpent crept towards her.

BOG SERPENT. 'Tis foolish you are, and ugly and weak.
*(The SERPENT slithers around her.)*

SEANACHAI 3. I will have this foot of mine mended, she thought.

SEANACHAI 1. The Serpent circled 'round and around and around...

*(...curls over the backs of her legs and slides around like a slick and slimy belt at her waist.)*

BOG SERPENT. 'Tis foolish you are, and ugly and weak!

SEANACHAI 2. I will have an ordinary foot like ordinary children, she thought.

SEANACHAI 3. Closer and closer until...

*(Now does slither over her shoulders.)*

BOG SERPENT. 'Tis foolish you are, and ugly and weak!

SEANACHAI 1. They were face to face, its fangs dripping with venom, tongue wagging...

*(And now, its head is raised high, staring down at her, emitting an awful hiss. Quick and strong and straight, BRIGID's hands reach up and grab the SERPENT's tongue. The glorious moment is held. BRIGID remains strong and straight as the huge SERPENT struggles against captivity, until it, like she, is motionless. The HERON and MARTEN have snuck back on, amazed.)*

HERON. She's done it.

MARTEN. No one's ever...she's tamed the Serpent!

BRIGID. What next?

SEANACHAI 3. What next?

SEANACHAI 1. What next?

HERON/MARTEN. Let...go...of its tongue. Wait! Wait! *(They back up all the way to the edge of the stage, then say:)* Now!

*(A beat, everyone is still, then BRIGID lets go of the SERPENT's tongue. The SERPENT doesn't move.)*

BRIGID. Oh, my! N-Now what?!
SEANACHAI 1. You know in your brain...
SEANACHAI 2. ...You know in your heart...
SEANACHAI 3. You know in your skin and your bones...
SEANACHAI/ALL. You'll not ever be the same...
SEANACHAI 1. That "Brigid" will forevermore mean "strength."
SEANACHAI 2. That "Shawn" will forevermore mean "one of a kind."
SEANACHAI 3. Brigid Shawn O'Grady, you know *now*...
BRIGID. Yes.
HERON. ...What you are destined to do.
MARTEN. What?
BRIGID. This!

*(BRIGID whips around onto the back of the SERPENT. She points the Bard's Rod. The SERPENT flies her over the bog, carrying a triumphant BRIGID with him.)*

HERON. Oh my! 'Tis flying.
MARTEN. Never saw the like.
MARTEN/HERON. And the girl astride!
HERON. 'Tis a wonder.
MARTEN. 'Tis a sight.
SEANACHAI 1. Over the bog and farther still.

SEANACHAI 2. Over tall juniper trees.

SEANACHAI 3. Over the rivers Brosna and Shannon.

SEANACHAI 1. Into the pillow-puffs of clouds and higher.

SEANACHAI/ALL. As far as they can go.

*(The SERPENT alights. BRIGID climbs off the SER-PENT. She walks away from it toward the small pond.)*

BRIGID *(tapping and chanting)*. "Tap once, twice, thrice/ Bard's Rod, point the way to the Well at World's Edge/ Point the way to what I need/ Point the way."

*(Under the keen eye of SEA MITHER, behind BRIGID, the SERPENT transforms into the SAGE. BRIGID twirls around until the rod, like the needle of a compass, points across the stage exactly as in the opening scene. BRIGID crosses to him.)*

BRIGID *(with wonder)*. You! You're the Sage!

SAGE. Yes, I am the Sage you seek. Welcome, Brigid Sean O'Grady.

BRIGID. You know my name?

SAGE. And your destiny.

BRIGID. To change this misshapen foot of mine to be like my other, and like everyone else's. I have passed the test of three.

SAGE. Yes. With an act of kindness for the Kelpie, which was a test of your heart.

BRIGID. And then, I did defeat the Giant.

SAGE. Very smart. A test of your mind.

BRIGID. And now, standing up to the deadly Bog Serpent...

SAGE. Indeed you did, passing the test of courage.

BRIGID. So. Here I am. At last. The Sea Mither promised to rid me of this ugly misshapen foot.

SAGE. Are you sure that's what you want?

BRIGID. Am I sure?

SAGE. I ask you to ask yourself.

BRIGID. Well. You know, no one noticed my foot amongst all the giants and mermaids and talking herons. And I did befriend the Kelpie, and I did outsmart a giant, and tamed the Bog Serpent.

SAGE. And that foot of yours?

BRIGID. Had nothing to do with it.

SAGE. A promise kept. I need only show you to yourself. *(Leads her to the Well:)* The magic of this well is its water. 'Tis a mirror showing you as you see yourself. Look now, at how you saw yourself before your journey.

BRIGID. That's me? I see a very large and ugly foot. 'Tis almost all of me.

SAGE. Look at how you see yourself *now*: *(Staring down at the Well, BRIGID smiles at herself.)* You see a kind and smart and brave person.

BRIGID. Yes, I do.

SAGE. And the foot?

BRIGID. The foot, is only one more part of who I am.

SAGE. A promise kept. The magic has happened.

BRIGID. It has. Thank you.

SAGE. You're the first child ever to reach me and this well. You have done a great thing, and we offer you our praise. Stay with us. And your difference will be no difference at all. You'll feast upon cakes and drink sweet nectar. Stay here with all the wonderful folk you have met. Play with the animals of our magical forests. Close your eyes and dream tales of wonder and beauty. *(BRIGID closes her eyes.)* 'Tis your choice to make.

BRIGID. But there is my mother and father, and the rivers and the hills of my County Clare.

SAGE. And a village where some will never understand, that will scorn and mock you. For some of them, different is frightful. Someone not like themselves is seen as something less. Oh my, you humans!...sometimes you make what's small seem so very big, and the big—your hearts and minds—almost nothing at all.

BRIGID *(thinks about it. Opens her eyes)*. I'll be going home.

SAGE. Brigid Shawn, take this rod again and tap three times. You'll find yourself back at the Cliffs of Moher.

*(As she taps three times, and emerging briefly from the assembled SEANACHAI, her friends bid her farewell.)*

HERON. Fare thee well.

MARTEN. Bye.

FARMER & FARMER'S WIFE. Do be safe, darlin'.

KELPIE. Need a hero, need a friend, call on me!

*(And her world transforms back to County Clare, back to her home.)*

SAGE. Tell of this journey of yours, the grown-ups in your life will not believe you.

*(Her MOTHER returns, carrying the bucket.)*

MOTHER. Five minutes and I still see a clean broom and dirty floor.

BRIGID. Five...minutes? But I...the Kelpie untied and talking, and the Giant ate griddlecakes, and the Serpent in the bog...

MOTHER. Ah, your daydreaming and book fancies.

*(BRIGID puts down the rod, and takes up her book. FA-THER enters.)*

BRIGID. No, 'tis a world of my possibilities. I'll be going to school, Mother. I need the learning, like everyone else—more than fairy tales. I'm ready for that now, and you must let me go.

FATHER. I'll not abide the village scoffing at my daughter because of that foot of yours.

BRIGID. It's their problem, I'll not make it mine. The foot is only one more part of who I am. Father, I'll be "little" no longer.

FATHER. A father must protect his child from the harsh world's harm.

BRIGID. You do. I carry your caring with me, Father, 'tis here *(her heart)* and here *(her head)*.

FATHER. It's time, then.

*(MOTHER and FATHER watch closely as...book in hand, BRIGID leaves home. MOTHER sees the Bard's Rod, holds it up in curiosity and wonder...)*

MOTHER. What in the world might *this* be?

*(BRIGID approaches the school. Before it stands the TOWNSPEOPLE. In the background are the SEANA-CHAI.)*

TAILOR. Not pretty at all.
SCHOOLTEACHER. Twisted inside and out.
BAKER. A mistake.
STREET CLEANER. Doesn't belong.

*(The LITTLE GIRL pushes through from behind them.)*

LITTLE GIRL. Hi. Remember me? My name's Brianna. What's yours? *(She holds out her hand. BRIGID takes it.)*
SEANACHAI 1 *(to audience).* "Brigid" will forever mean "strength"…
SEANACHAI 2 *(to audience).* …And "Shawn" will forever mean "one of a kind."
SEANACHAI 3 *(to audience).* Years and years to come, her own child will pick up the Bard's Rod and feel the magic of it and point the way of possibilities…
SEANACHAI 2. …of hopes…
SEANACHAI 1. …and of dreams.
BRIGID. My name is Brigid Shawn O'Grady.

*(And the two of them—BRIGID and the LITTLE GIRL—walk through the TOWNSPEOPLE toward the schoolhouse door as the SCHOOLTEACHER extends a hand in welcome.)*

**CURTAIN**

# DIRECTOR'S NOTES

# DIRECTOR'S NOTES